SPARKLE OF LOVE

Written and Illustrated by:
Nora Bunn

Sparkle of Love

Copyright © 2024 by Nora Bunn. All rights reserved.

No rights claimed for public domain material, all rights reserved. No parts of this publication may be reproduced, stored in any retrieval system, or transmitted in any form or by any means, electronic, mechanical, recording, or otherwise, without the prior written permission of the author. Violations may be subject to civil or criminal penalties.

ISBN:
978-1-63308-762-0 (paperback)
978-1-63308-763-7 (ebook)

Cover and Interior Design by *R'tor John D. Maghuyop*
Illustrated by *Nora Bunn*

CHALFANT ECKERT
PUBLISHING

PO Box 1665, Rolla MO 65402

Printed in United States of America

SPARKLE OF LOVE

Written and Illustrated by:
Nora Bunn

DEDICATION

To Reese and Jack - I love you.

You're my favorites.

Heart Lover lives in the most magical place on earth...

Until one day, that all changed.

Heart Lover found herself having to go to the hospital
for something that was in her horn.

She took a rainbow cloud all the way to the hospital
with mom and dad. When she got there, the rainbow turned
into thunderstorms.

Dr. Gatey searched and searched for answers until
she realized that Heart Lover needed new uni-cells in her body
to fight what they call "the owie in her horn".

Heart Lover was devastated knowing her birthday was coming up
and she didn't want to be in a hospital for her special day!

Dr. Gatey, Nurse Lavey, and Dazzle took good care of Heart Lover, but she could not stop thinking about her birthday next week!

How can the hospital let unicorns miss their birthdays?

Then came the day that Heart Lover received her uni-cells.

Dr. Gatey was hoping that Heart Lover would smile to know that she would feel so much better, but instead, her tail turned from bright red to brown and the sparkle on Heart Lover's body started to shed away.

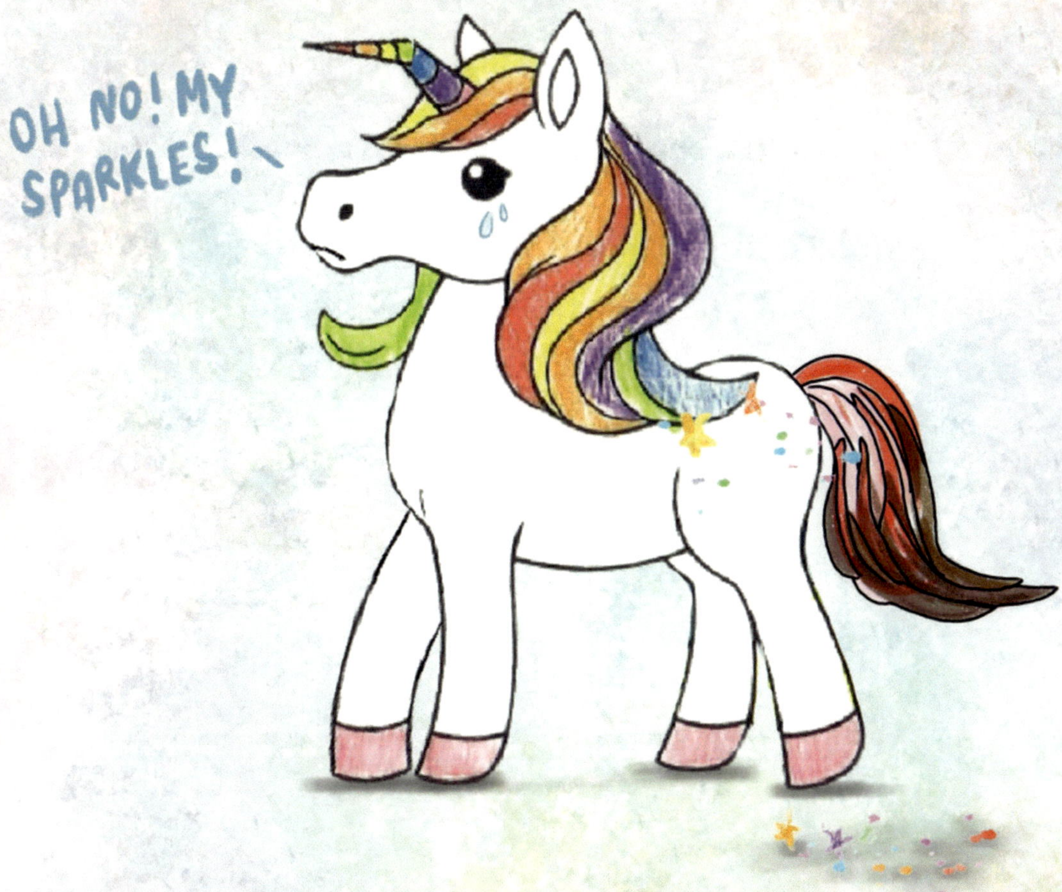
OH NO! MY SPARKLES!

One day mom brought in Heart Lovers' stuffed friends
and they cheered her up, but she was still scared
that she would miss her birthday.

Heart Lover's zebra friend, Dazzle, came into her room to plan
a birthday party for next week, but Heart Lover couldn't
come up with any good ideas.

With each passing day, Heart Lover's sparkle
would fall off her body one by one.

Then, two days before the big, special birthday,
Dazzle comes in again, different kinds of party horns in hand…

Rainbow polka dots, blue sparkles, lime green with daisies…
so many to choose from! Heart lover started trying all these different horns and the bright red color started to come back into her tail.

Plus, the sparkles appeared on her body again!

On the day of Heart Lover's birthday, she rested all morning long, feeling blue. While she was sleeping, Dr. Gatey, Nurse Lavey, Dazzle and all Heart Lover's stuffed animals decorated around her – filling her entire room with sparkle and rainbow colors.

Heart Lover opened her eyes to a HUGE birthday party and a sign on her wall that said...

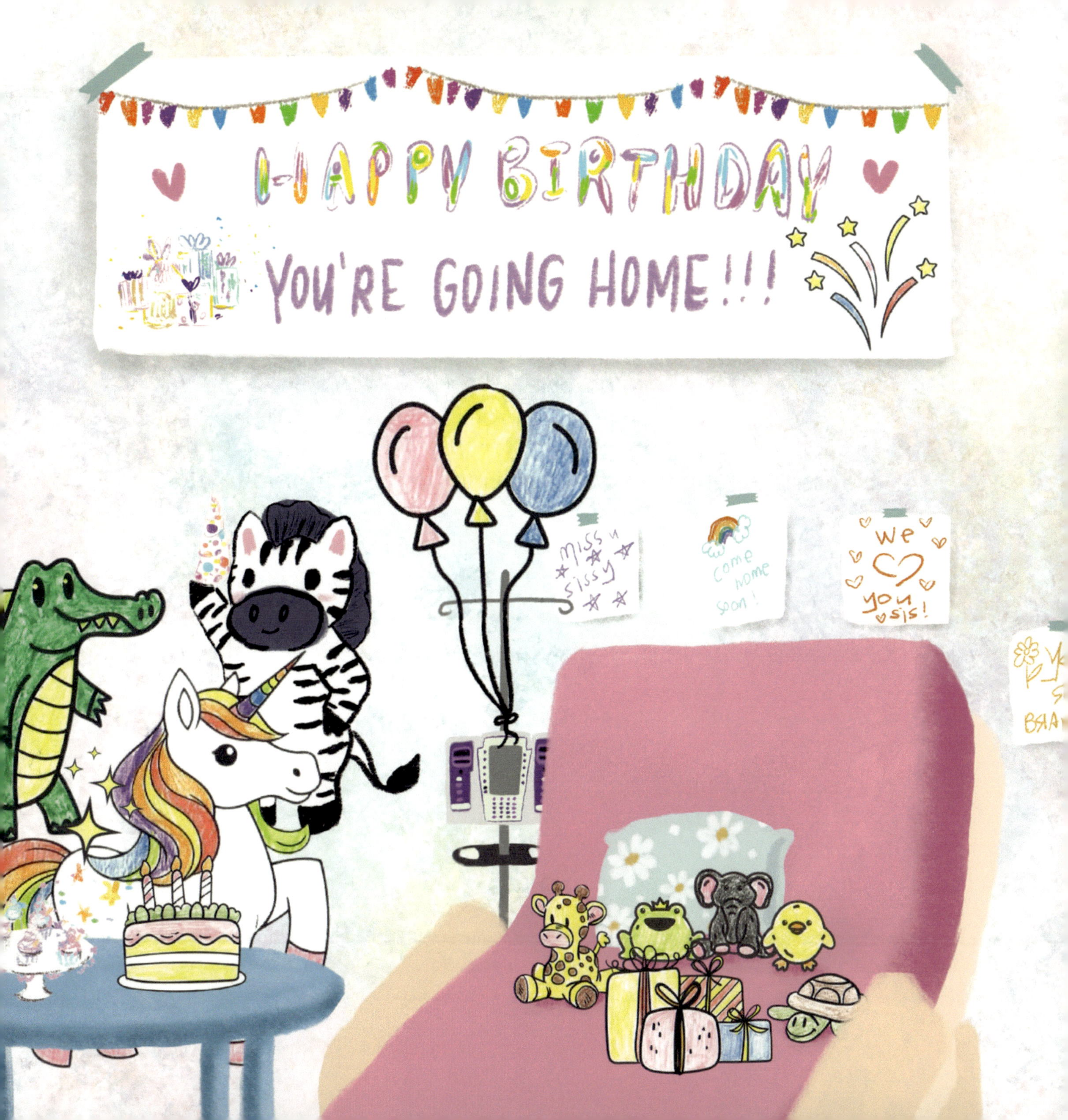

Heart Lover jumped with joy! Her wish had come true.

When Heart Lover arrived home, all her friends and family, including her brother and sister, were cheering and waving.

There was a sparkle of hope waiting for Heart Lover at home.

Made in the USA
Columbia, SC
26 July 2025